IN MAMMON WE TRUST . . .

IN
MAMMON

WE TRUST . . .

Al Staggs

RESOURCE *Publications* • Eugene, Oregon

Resource Publications
A division of Wipf and Stock Publishers
199 W 8th Ave, Suite 3
Eugene, OR 97401

In Mammon We Trust
By Staggs, Al
Copyright©2011 by Staggs, Al
ISBN 13: 978-1-5326-5542-5
Publication date 5/2/2018
Previously published by The Intermudia Press, 2011

In loving memory of Carol

and with love to Ryan, Jenn, Liana, Maya, Rebekah, Matty, Jakob, Miah, Austin, Christa, Lisa and Martha.

PREFACE

Although the disparity between the wealthiest Americans and the middle and poorer classes increased sharply during the Reagan years, the primary cause of our nation's current economic condition can be attributed to the policies of the Bush administration. The Bush tax cuts were structured to disproportionately favor wealthy Americans, and the wars in Iraq and Afghanistan have proven to be both ill-advised and exorbitantly expensive. Due to the decrease in revenue resulting from the millionaires' tax cuts, the cost of the wars has created the enormous deficit that we now face.

The gap between the rich and poor continues to grow at an alarming rate and the middle class is becoming smaller. I am convinced that people of the Christian faith cannot continue talking about spirituality without also talking about the theological meaning of our present economic plight. Liturgy, worship, prayer, praise, meditation and Bible study are missing the mark unless they include an examination of what our Christian faith means in the face of an oppressive economic system that unjustly benefits the wealthy and penalizes and oppresses the poor and middle classes.

I have been writing reflections on issues related to the spirituality of economics for almost a decade, and in the midst of the continued economic decline over the last four years I found new inspiration from the writings of Walter Rauschenbusch and William Stringfellow. Rauschenbusch reminded the generation of a previous Gilded Age that scripture does in fact speak to the issues of greed and poverty. Stringfellow was adept in reminding us that any discussion of spirituality should always be bound up with the real problems that people are forced to confront every day.

Until we Christians take seriously the desperate circumstances that many face on a daily basis, much of our Christianity is merely form without substance and relevance. The question that we confront is not whether we believe in the veracity of our scriptures, but whether we can apply those scriptures to the economic and political structures that shape our lives.

If you are wealthy, you are living in the Golden Age of your American Dream, and it's a damned fine time to be alive. The two major political parties are working hammer and tong to bless you and keep you. The laws are being re-written—often by fiat, and in defiance of court orders—to strengthen the walls separating you and your wealth from the motley masses. Your stock portfolio, mostly made by and for oil and war, continues to swell. Your banks and Wall Street shops destroyed the economy for everyone except you, and not only did they get away with it, but were handed a vast dollop of taxpayer cash as a bonus prize.

— William Rivers Pitt

The number of billionaires in the United States increased by 19% between 2007 and 2008. During that same period the number of Americans living in poverty increased by 2.5 million.

A person must completely close his eyes on his morals, that in a Christian society so filled with people in need, there are other people who are so proud to have great wealth.

— Leo Tolstoy

IN
MAMMON

WE TRUST . . .

IN MAMMON WE TRUST

Most of our god-talk only serves as a mask
since it is money that drives every one of us.
The dollar is always the bottom line
and it is the tally sheet of who we are
as individuals and as a society.

The dollar is the great motivator,
the Great Spirit that causes us
to rise early and go to bed late,
thinking about our bank balances
and our debts, or what we'll have
when we retire from our current labors
to support ourselves and our families.

If God were a part of our nation's economic plan,
there would be no poverty,
millions of children would not go to bed hungry,
everyone would have access to health care.
The real crisis in our Dollar Theology
is that most of us don't even care
about the fact that a small faction
in our *democracy* has rigged capitalism
into a distorted socialism for the rich.

So let's eradicate the lies
that are inscribed on our coinage
and put instead the inscription
"In Mammon We Trust."
Let us be honest in our evil
and truthful about the actual god
of this richest of earthly empires.

CAPITALISM ON TRIAL

When the wealthiest 1% of Americans
own nearly 50% of our nation's wealth,
something is wrong, dreadfully wrong.

When 45,000,000 people are uninsured
in the wealthiest nation in the world,
and when more than 40,000 Americans
die each year due to lack of insurance coverage,
something is woefully wrong,
manifestly unjust.

When the average corporate executive earns
hundreds of times more than the average worker,
in addition to receiving extra millions in bonuses,
that is unbridled avarice.

When the economic system is skewed
so that profits are funneled up
to the multi-millionaires and to
gigantic corporations that pay little if any taxes
instead of "trickling down"
to the middle class and poor,
that is robbery—legalized theft.

When health care companies practice policies
that refuse to pay legitimate claims
while paying huge bonuses to their executives
and huge profits to their stockholders,
that is injustice, plain and simple.

When wars are never ceased
due to "American interests"
(oil and/or profits for our
military-industrial complex)
and our soldiers on the ground
and citizens of the invaded nations
continue to suffer death,
dismemberment, trauma and disease,
that's predatory capitalism at its worst.

Capitalism, as it has been practiced
since the Reagan years,
has profited the few on the backs
of the many—the middle class and the poor.
Socialism was craftily compared
to communism
and became such a bad word
that many of those who need
a helping hand from the government
regularly go to the polls
and vote against their own interests.

It is past time to put capitalism on trial
and to reshape this golden calf
to make possible the fair sharing of wealth.
For there is no freedom
without economic justice.

Put no value on earthly things, which worms and rust consume, and which thieves break into and steal. Rather, y'all set your hearts on spiritual values, which neither worms nor rust consume, and which thieves do not break into and steal. For your values and your character are wrapped up together.

— Matthew 6:19–21, Clarence Jordan's "Cotton Patch Gospel"

BUDGET CUTS

The Grand Old Party and the Tea Party
demand that the millionaires be afforded
every opportunity to keep partying
in the manner to which they have become accustomed.

Medicare, as well as Medicaid, must go.
Public Broadcasting must go.
National Public Radio must go.
The Environmental Protection Agency must go.
Community health centers must go.
Home heating assistance for the poor must go.
Planned Parenthood must go.
(All babies must be born, of course, but then forgotten.)
Pell grants and funding for public education must go.
Collective bargaining for workers' rights must go.
Social Security must go.
And so it goes.

Should excessive funding for the war machine go? No!
Too many multi-millionaires own stock in the
corporations that amass huge profits through
the production of weapons of mass destruction.

Should government subsidies of the oil companies go? No!
Their annual profits that are currently in the billions
might be reduced to mere millions.

Should the disproportionately large tax cuts for the wealthy go? No!
Our wealthy masters need the tax cuts
to maintain their status quo,
to fund the election campaigns of their minions,
to spend boatloads of cash helping GOP governors
crush the working people in their states.

And so it goes.
Everything must go.
Everything, that is, which benefits average Americans
but is not needed by the wealthiest among us.

THE TEA PARTY FARCE

Fancying themselves as modern-day prototypes
of the Bostonians who centuries ago
defied the British Empire,
these older, white, government-subsidized,
corporately-funded heroes and heroines
bravely take on the enemy of government spending.

Tea Partyers are the paradoxical people
who decry socialism on the way to the bank
to deposit their Social Security checks,
with their Medicare cards
tucked securely in their wallets.
They have all they need
and can't see beyond their own noses.
They are loud for their number
and equally obnoxious.

Homogeneous by definition,
the Tea Partyers hanker for life
as it was back in the "good old days"
when everyone knew their places
and the entitled were safe from having to share
our nation's goods and services with
the second-class citizens.

Tea Partyers like to drive
but they don't want to pay the toll.
It takes a lot of money to run a government
but the Tea Partyers don't want to pay taxes
to keep our roads and bridges safe,
to modernize our infrastructure,

to protect our environment,
to provide health care options for those
who cannot pay the ever-rising costs of insurance.
And heaven forbid that their corporate masters
should be required to pitch in their fair share.

They are prostitutes who have gone a-whoring
with the greediest among us—Murdoch,
the Koch brothers and their like—who
believe that no industry should be regulated
and that our government "of the people,
by the people, and for the people"
should be starved of the resources it needs
to provide services for the people.

The Tea Partyers are paving the way for revolution
but not the revolution they are seeking.
The impending revolution will leave these angry,
loud-mouthed, selfish drum beaters in the dust
created by the tens of millions who will some day
find their voice, their solidarity, and make
the current Tea Party movement seem
as distant as that Tea Party in 1773.

WHAT GOD HATH NOT WROUGHT

The magnificent symbols of our faith,
those tall steeples that dot our cities
were built by money
and by our assumption
that they would serve as a reminder
of the place of our faith
amidst the places of commerce.
God did not create those edifices.
We did.

And it is those massive structures,
the sanctuaries and steeples,
along with our belief
that God inspired them
and that he is in our midst,
which indict us.
For the hungry continue to beg,
to seek food, jobs, dignity
under the shadows of the imposing
symbols of our faith.

The richest 5 percent of Americans now hold 63.5 percent of the nation's wealth, the Economic Policy Institute estimated last week, about five times more than the 12.8 percent share that belongs to the bottom 80 percent.

(March 2011)

PARADIGM SHIFT

What if the currency of our work
was service and not selfishness,
if we could give more to the needy
and keep less for ourselves?
What if the public welfare
was more important than private enrichment,
if corporations considered
the Common Good as their bottom line,
and if our worth was not measured
by our financial holdings
but rather by what we contributed to society?

It's only a dream, just a dream now,
but hopefully our grandchildren will inherit
the realization of such a vision.

GANGSTAS OF WALL STREET

Like drug lords of Mexico or Columbia
these titans of business
own huge estates, private jets
and priceless works of art.
Yet, unlike the crimes of the drug czars,
their crimes do not involve bloodshed.
Weapons are not needed to secure
and maintain their opulent lifestyles.

The magnates have no fear
that their financial interests
will ever be endangered,
for they hold the purse strings,
and those who write our laws
are in their pockets.

Yes, there is immorality in the system
but the press will not print it,
the broadcast media will not report it,
the government is hamstrung
by deep-pocketed lobbyists,
and the church is complicit in the injustice
by looking the other way.

The gangstas of Wall Street
are flexing their muscles
and the good guys are cowering
either in resignation or hopelessness.
When will it end?
How will it end?

HOW MUCH FAITH?

So how much faith do we possess?
From where does our financial security come?
The economic crisis has deeply touched
both our emotional and spiritual lives
and we are compelled to ask deep questions.
If our lifestyles are radically altered; that is,
if our houses, cars and most of our possessions are lost
and our savings and retirement accounts become depleted
and we can no longer afford health coverage,
in what fashion will we then pray
and what will be the nature of our worship,
our praise and our thanksgiving to God?

Might all those turn to laments,
the kind of laments that the vast majority
of people throughout the world
have voiced for centuries?
They knew the grinding lifestyle of poverty
long before the sin of avarice gave birth
to our own present crisis.

The minister who really follows the mind of Christ will likely take the side of the poor in most issues. Yet, in so many situations, pastors either take the side of the more wealthy or else they remain silent or neutral, which is an impossible position to take.

— Walter Rauschenbusch

ASSAULT OF POVERTY

Poverty assails and allows no provisions
for body, mind and soul—
a condition that feels like
a judgment from God.
To be bereft of money for necessities
is to be victimized by a system
that is no respecter of persons,
or only of those who have played their cards
right to acquire their disproportionate gain.

Our economic status quo is violent.
It is torture, aided and abetted
by government and the high courts.
Democracy is a farce.
Capitalism prostitutes and persecutes,
taking resources and allowing the few
to hoard that which was intended
for the common good.

Poor, poor people and no one
is there for them.
Those who attempt to speak for them
are ignored and ridiculed.
God is worshipped faithfully
in our temples of capitalism
where the moneychangers
have set up their shops,
but that God cannot
save the poor among us
for Pharaoh maintains the reins
of power and the control of their lives.

WHAT DO YOU THINK
ABOUT THAT?

GE, the nation's largest corporation,
paid no taxes last year.
Defense contractors are getting rich
by helping to establish "democracy"
in faraway oil-rich nations.
What do you think about that?

Here at home, tens of millions
struggle to survive on beggars' wages.
As their homes are taken,
rent prices escalate
to take advantage of the situation.
For the uninsured there are no visits
to the dentist or doctor,
only the possibility of an undetected illness
that could drive them into eternal debt.
What do you think about that?

Or do you have little time
to think about the structure of our lives,
a structure that is not of our making?
What do you think about?
Oh, the distractions of our petty interests
as we get our news from distorted sources
who tell us what they want us to hear
with no regard to the veracity of their spin.

And we go on refusing to face the truth
about the evil and greedy structures
that have enslaved the vast majority of our citizens.
Some attend churches that mostly focus
on what happened centuries ago,
and they have not a clue as to the application
of the texts of which they speak and sing.
The routine of living has its own agenda
that leaves us ignorant and apathetical
regarding our own plight.
What do you think about that?
What do you think about that?

Avarice, the spur of industry.

— David Hume

Poverty is the parent of revolution and crime.

— Aristotle

FOREBODING FUTURE

It's Dickensesque.
When there are so many with too little
and too few with too much,
that's the kind of condition
that fostered the French Revolution.
The structures of laws, customs,
policies and business as usual
could one day be disrupted by marches,
strikes, protests and even violence
growing out of a universal sense of despair.

A system that habitually and legally
rewards the rich at the expense of the poor
is not moral and should no longer be legal.
We're not living in another Great Depression.
This is the Great Oppression.

For the present to change might require
an upheaval the likes of which this nation
has never before experienced.

Eventually, inevitably, a bold change
must be forced upon the system
because politicians and their corporate donors
will never willingly agree
to the major reversals that are required
to reduce the great financial gap
between the rich and the poor.

Capitalism, the free enterprise system,
is increasingly on the hot seat.
Trickle down has trickled out.
There's less for charity, but charity
was never the answer to this disparity anyway.

And the churches with overhead expenses
that always mandate budgets that reflect
mere pocket change to human need
are now being required to cut even deeper
into those meager allotments.
The churches are trapped by their financial structures
and by maintenance of the houses in which
they meet to pay homage to a God who
most certainly has a preferential option for the poor.

REPUBLICAN BASE

To think that this is the party of Lincoln
is unimaginable, unthinkable.
This party of so-called *moral values*
has deteriorated to the party
of racists, greedy adulterers,
obstructionists of reasonable legislation.
When sworn into office,
they place their right hands on the Bible
while their left hands are groping
for the cash of lobbyists.
These are the minions of Rush
who heel and kneel at that
big, fat idiot's every command.

The members of this Sold-Out Party
would do well to take a field trip
to the Lincoln Memorial
and stand beneath that imposing statue
of the man who was a giant
for his time and for all time,
in order to be reminded just how small
they and their party are in our time.
The "base" of the Republican Party
reeks of white entitlement,
reminiscent of a segregated America
and a male-dominated ruling class.
It's not the America I desire.

DISCOMFORTING WORSHIP

Sitting in a church pew Sunday
after Sunday can be painful.
No, the cushions are comfortable enough.
It's just that the rituals, prayers, songs
and sermons seem so ahistorical.
"Nothing is controversial,"
I think to myself as my gaze falls
upon that most controversial Cross
that hangs conspicuously at the
center of our place of worship.

In avoiding mention of the present crises,
have our songs and prayers
become hollow, shallow shibboleths
that merely provide personal consolation
for our individual lives and concerns?

The announcement time indicates
that the windows of the church
are tightly shut, for we appear
to be obsessed with our hubbub
of activities and churchly matters
while an earthly hell is erupting around us.

Yes, the services provide us an opportunity
to reflect on the eternal perspective,
that this life is but a small part
of what awaits us in the promise of heaven.
But is this an avoidance of the here and now,
the present, this life, the life of our Jesus,
whose 33 years were a pivotal time in human history?

Uttering the words of the Lord's Prayer makes me squirm.
"Thy kingdom come, thy will be done
on earth as it is in Heaven."
And I wonder how many of us actually realize
the significance of the words we are reciting.
And I wonder to what degree I, or any of us,
believe that it is our duty to endeavor to make
this a reality here on earth in our own time.

Receiving communion gives me cause to ponder,
"Am I really willing to take this cup of suffering
with Jesus, or is this just another numbing ritual
to me, a ritual that has little relevance to the need
to work for the causes of peace and justice
that were at the core of his teachings?"

So this is a confession of guilt
and also an expression of desire
that my worship, our worship, might become
more than a demonstration of our adoration of God.
My hope is that it might also provoke
all of us to think of the suffering world
around us and remember that Jesus
lived and died for this world of today.

Avarice is always poor.

— Samuel Johnson

Poverty wants much, but avarice everything.

— Publius Syrus

A PERSON'S WORTH

A beggar man on the street
eyes a quarter on the sidewalk
as an unexpected treasure.
His net worth has now risen from zero
to twenty-five cents.

A stockbroker cashes in on a "hot" stock,
netting another twenty grand or so;
all in a day's work.
It's a tough life but someone has to live it.
He'll use the gain to purchase a new Rolex—
expensive, but appropriate
for a man of his status.
Too bad none of his capital gains
will buy him any more time on earth
to accumulate additional wealth.

The beggar man is worth a quarter of a dollar;
the broker's worth is measured in millions.
And so it is in the Land of Free Enterprise
and the Home of the Poverty-Stricken.

ECONOMIC MADNESS

Times are tough
with our economy in shambles
and with the loss of jobs,
steady paychecks and benefits.
The plight of the unemployed
and the underemployed
keeps them awake at night,
wondering how the bills
and obligations will be paid.

Insecurity, anxiety, depression
manifest themselves in the homes
of those who are struggling to make ends meet.
Their sense of self-worth has been sorely damaged
since their work, their livelihood, is gone
and with it the ability to provide for those
whose welfare depends on them.

This epidemic of loss—loss of job,
loss of income, loss of retirement—
inflicts deep wounds of discouragement
in the hearts of those affected.
Their effort to maintain some semblance
of a lifestyle that offers dignity
is an exercise in futility.
The future looks bleak, foreboding.
Hope is being strained to the limit.

The greed of a tiny minority,
people in places of power and influence,
has created this financial nightmare
that attacks the very fabric of our nation.
The plight of the erstwhile middle class,
to say nothing of the poor,
is an indictment of our free enterprise system
that rewards the avaricious people
at the top of the corporate ladders
whose insatiable craving for wealth
fuels their evil practices that condemn
their fellow citizens to live
in states of hopelessness and fear.

No Avarice Anonymous support group exists
to assist the super-rich in overcoming
their intoxication with exorbitant wealth,
and there is no desire to create one.
They don't want to concern themselves with
the level of devastation they are creating
through their outsourcing of jobs,
the interest rates they impose on credit,
their inflated salaries, bonuses and perks.

This ghastly aberration of capitalism
has failed our country miserably.
Greed always extracts a price
and the American public is picking up this tab.

It's time for real change,
change that will return this nation's wealth
to the hands of the many, where it belongs.

Some day, hopefully sooner rather than later,
a much different paradigm of economics will destroy,
demolish this form of torture that,
on the surface, has no hint of violence.

May there soon be a day when the great majority
of this nation will rise up together and remind
those in the halls of Congress, and the Fortune Makers
who arc guilty of creating this financial monster,
that we will no longer accept this system.

In order to stop the madness, we will, as a nation
goverened by the people and for the people,
resist and rebel in a multitude of ways
in order to make our message loud and clear.

We are coming closer and closer to the brutal equation that one person's wealth is another's poverty. Riches held are riches withheld.

— Bruce C. Birch & Larry L. Rasmussen,
"The Predicament of the Prosperous"

POOR LEISURE

For the increasing number of persons
who have less to live on
and less to spend for clothes, food,
excursions with the family,
and much needed medical care,
leisure means watching the tube
and viewing commercials
advertising things they cannot afford.

It's seeing from the outside
the lifestyles of the rich and famous
and hearing views from news pundits
who have no clue what it means
to do without.

And then there are the sports channels.
Professional athletes make more money
in one year than a poor family
will make in a lifetime.

Poor Leisure.
If the best things in life are free,
the poor should know this
better than anyone else.

GIVING TO GOD

Walking to church a few weeks ago
I was approached by a beggar
who asked if I could spare some change
to help him get through the day.
Even though we were both
walking in the same direction,
I knew it was not likely that he
was planning to worship at my church.

In my pocket I was carrying a check
that represented my tithe for the month.
Almost impulsively, I gave him
the exact amount of money in cash
that I had intended to give
to my church in the form of a check.
And I gave the money to the beggar
with the full realization
that by this act I was truly giving
my monthly portion to God.

BIRTH OF A KINGDOM?

If only I could remember
what the birth of that child,
the baby Jesus,
born two thousand years ago,
really means to me, to all of us
who annually commemorate his birth.

That child was born
in the context of poverty—
a refugee, an immigrant.

Marked for a most radical
mission to challenge the powers
of both religion and state,
that child would subsequently be
victimized by both.

His mother provided a glimpse of his
radical purpose by uttering that the rich
shall be brought low and the poor lifted up.
And what could that mean today
in this nation of the super-rich
with the vast number of impoverished?

I'm caring less for all of the traditional
trappings of the season of Christmas,
and I yearn to catch sight of something more
to be associated with the birth of Jesus.

I'd prefer to think of the Christmas season
as a new promise of the coming of the Kingdom of God
on earth as it is in heaven.
The baby was and still is the promise of a new order,
not just a symbol of a religious or cultural celebration.

A new order is needed—an order that confronts
our own powers of religion and state.
The baby Jesus is a reminder that Kingdom Work
is ongoing, unfinished and waiting,
in our own time, to find fulfillment.

Augustine said that a person who possesses a surplus possesses the goods of others; in other words, if you've got too much, you're a thief!

— Clarence Jordan

QUIET VIOLENCE

Structures of gross inequality
push their weight against our citizens.
Freedom is only a word, not a reality.
Capitalism is holding liberty hostage.
Lower our flags to half mast,
for symbolism without substance
is a farce and a tragedy.

The most damaging violence in this society
comes from the perpetrators
of its lethal structures of tax cuts,
hedge funds, prime mortgages,
inflated incomes and excessive luxury
for those perpetrators, the super-rich,
while the rest of us are powerless
to change our economic fate.

Financial structures of this nature
are always legal, though seldom moral.
It boils down to 21st Century slavery,
and perhaps only another civil war
could free the economically enslaved
from this extraordinary and cruel inequality.

SOUL SATISFACTION

My soul cannot seem to grasp
that which my hands clutch so dearly.
The soul is not satisfied by possessions
or by the desire to acquire more things.
The life within is not easily assuaged
and there is no need to search
for that which cannot satisfy.

Yet I acquire and I desire more
and remain impoverished in spirit.
There is nothing I own or might own
that could be exchanged for the intangible,
priceless life of the soul.

SOME DAY

Some day
when wars cease
and the flag of peace
is firmly planted in every land . . .

Some day
when all God's children
can go to bed without hunger
and their parents can sleep without anxiety . . .

Some day
when the rule of profit
will not enslave our time and labor,
when the worth of a person will no longer be measured by wealth . . .

Some day
when the sick of every nation will be cared for
without thought for material gain . . .

Some day
when the environment will be protected instead of violated,
when it will rightly be seen as God's gift to us
and not as our possession to casually neglect and destroy . . .

Some day . . . some day.
O Lord, may that day come soon
when all the world will be warmed by your strength and grace
and your children will live together in peace,
tolerance and compassion for one another.

When that day comes, there will be no distinction
between rich and poor
and we will find our home and security
in your Kingdom on earth.

THE ROOT OF IT ALL

And we all participate,
by necessity,
in the pursuit of money
to earn our keep,
to pay our bills,
to pay the taxes
that are gathered
disproportionately
from those who can
least afford to pay.
And those tax dollars
are increasingly spent
on instruments of death
rather than on life-saving
measures to aid the needy.

And we live in
a state of denial
in this *free* nation,
refusing to recognize
both the disparity
and the destruction
that are the result
of the government-
sanctioned violence
being perpetrated upon us
without weapons.

In plain truth, it is not want, but rather abundance, that creates avarice.

— Montaigne

ECONOMICS OF DRINKING

My daddy usually saved
his drinking binges
for the Christmas season.
About a week before Christmas Day
he would be dragged into our house,
stone-cold drunk, by his friends.

He was a man who didn't drink socially
and never imbibed any other time of the year.
When I was older, he confided to me
that what motivated him to drink
was the thought that he could never adequately
provide for the five of us, his children.
Of course, the drinking didn't help
our family's financial woes.
But it afforded him at least
a week or two of mental respite
from his feelings of inadequacy.

And this phenomenon
repeats itself in family after family
where alcohol serves as the drug of choice
to assuage the side effects of poverty.

Poverty and alcohol are deadly twin sisters
that affect the pocketbooks,
the lives, the souls
of our nation's poor.

'TIS THE SEASON

How ironic it is,
in this nation of countless churches,
that the fattest business profits
accrue during the season
that celebrates the birth
of a child who was born in poverty,
a child who would one day
cast the moneychangers
out of the temple,
a child who would preach
good news to the poor
and liberation to the oppressed,
a child who would die
in poverty by the hand of the state.

DECEPTION OF TRUTH

Truth lies hidden
beneath mountains of words,
doctrines, beliefs and lifestyles
that obliquely prevent the practice
of compassion and justice
in this "land of opportunity."

Our nation's politicians and political policies
are bought and sold on the market.
Violence against the poor and the middle class
is most insidious and cruel in the halls of Congress,
where our elected officials prostitute themselves
to the highest bidders while the poor cannot find an advocate
who is rich enough to buy a voice in the nation's capital.

Truth lies hidden beneath a façade of religiosity
in this very Christian land where churches worship
faithfully and impressively each weekend
while sponsoring a few mission projects
and giving alms to a few of the poor,
though not working to effect any change
in the political and economic structure that breeds our poor.

God is praised and the poor are forgotten.
Blasphemy is rampant in our congregations.
Praise the Lord!
Praise the Lord!
Praise the Lord?

Perhaps it is time to mute our voices of praise,
to cease our ecstatic singing,
and to forego the reading of scripture
until we can recognize that the church was intended to relate
to the human tragedies being played out
all around our holy walls,
our bastions of "holiness."

Capitalism and false Christianity—
burying Truth under whitewashed lies.

THE CURSE UPON US

The curse upon us
is not from God.
It is the result
of a feeding frenzy
by the privileged few.

A tiny, wealthy minority
has been systematically
stealing from the national treasury
and from the pocketbooks
of America's hard-working,
tax-paying women and men.

Those über-wealthy folk
have robbed the rest of us
of our livelihoods,
our lifestyles,
not with weapons
but with the aid of
a derelict Congress
originally elected
to represent all of us.

A nation that puts so much stress on getting ahead has a hard time dealing with those who fall behind. If you're successful, you seldom identify with failure. This is proved by the fact that integration of races has already resulted in an even greater segregation by class. The so-called underclass has all the markings of a subordinate caste. In the long run, I believe, class will prove a tougher nut to crack than race.

— William Sloane Coffin

MAMMON THE GOD

That which is universally omnipotent is money.
All of life is based upon wages,
debts and the balance sheet.
Even the magnificent edifices
erected to symbolize God's presence
in our cities and countryside
are constructed and maintained
by the contribution of money.

We are a Capitalist nation,
not a Christian nation.
The crosses that grace
our grand houses of worship
stand in graphic contrast
to the architecture of the churches.
The very essence of the story
of the crucifixion of Jesus,
who died as an anti-hero
with no material "net worth,"
escapes so many who profess his name.

All that is tangible has a price, a cost.
We live in houses that demand payment
and so many of those are being threatened
as the foreclosures escalate at an alarming rate
while the wages and savings of the owners
are lost or in a rapid downward spiral.

Fuel, that runs our transportation,
takes ever more of our pay
as prices continue to soar,
while oil companies bask
in the knowledge that their profits
have never been better.

Mammon is our god.
We are totally dependent
on this deity who consumes
our time and demands more and more
of our lives in energy, devotion and stress.

Mammon's most ardent worshippers
are those who remain unmoved
in the comfort of their excessive wealth
while the vast majority of citizens
grow old before their time,
having to "make do" and pretend
this is the way things are supposed to be.

What controls and operates everything,
the wheels of all our lives and activities,
is the dollar, the almighty dollar.

BIRTH OF A REVOLUTIONARY

Every Christmas my spiritual life dries up
and is blown by the winds as I observe
another orgy of purchasing, consuming,
decorating homes and businesses to disguise
the truth of the meaning of Christ's birth and life,
the truth about our utter poverty of spirituality.

There is no Good News for the poor
and there is no peace on earth
even though we have allocated tons of money,
that which could have aided the least among us,
for our arsenal of adult toys—weapons
created to insure security for our lifestyles
of get-all-you-can-while-you-can
and to hell with the rest of the world.

Christmas has become difficult to bear,
for our Christmas celebrations stand as a paradox
to the context of the birth of Jesus
and the promise of the Kingdom of God on earth.
It is a burden to hear passages from the gospel of Luke,
a most radical document,
the way we recite it, as though the passages
have relevance in our splendid houses of worship,
those places where we sing our joyful songs
in mockery of the inequity, injustice
and violence in our midst.

Jesus stood firmly against inequity, injustice and violence.
So I cannot celebrate the spirit of Christmas
without remembering that Christmas is about
the birth of a Revolutionary.

SPIRITUALITY FROM BELOW

Into the sanctuary they file
with heads bowed,
hoping to catch a glimpse of the eternal,
something that will place
their present struggles in perspective.
The days, weeks, months and years
are long and grueling.
So, on this day of rest,
meaning is sought for the drudgery
of their labors and lives.

Singing is both mournful and joyful.
It is dirge-like as they confront their crises
and it is exuberant
as they attempt to grasp the concept
that God is with them.
They realize in the depths of their being
that if God is with them
he must be sorrowful
and distressed, as they are.

Thus there is comfort and solace
for the downcast,
recognizing that the Creator is with them.
Sunday worship becomes cathartic,
a renewal of vision
and a renewal of joy
for those who have nothing else
on which they can lean their weary souls.

No one can serve two masters; for either he will hate the one and love the other, or else he will be loyal to the one and despise the other. You cannot serve God and mammon.

— Matthew 6:24

WHO HOLDS
THE PURSE STRINGS?

When it comes time for relief to Haiti,
who can spare the hundreds of millions
of dollars to make a dent in the
suffering and misery of a forgotten people?

When it comes to rebuilding devastated New Orleans,
who has the cash to rebuild the homes and lives
of those who suffered from nature's rage?

When health care is needed for tens of millions
across our wealthy nation,
who has the revenue required
to provide equitable health care for all?

Where is the line item in our nation's budget
for the homeless, the unemployed,
the penniless who reside so very close
to the affluent in our cities?

There's always money for war
and for the contractors whose enormous coffers
grow more bloated with each new conflict.

There's always money for the fat cats on Wall Street,
who systematically steal from the national treasury
and practice usury to the extreme.

There's only so much to go around,
so the forgotten in Haiti and New Orleans,
the sick, the homeless and the poor
will remain forgotten
because the devil holds the purse strings.

We give lip service to compassion,
but our spending priorities bear evidence that
compassion is not our business.
Thus we, as a nation, live in darkness
while too many of us profit
from the devil's disbursements.

CHURCH AND LIFE, THEN AND NOW

Going to church, I find the focus
on the *then* to the neglect of the *now*.
Upon returning home, I read the news
about our corrupt economic system,
our extravagant military spending
that takes funding from programs
that would benefit our citizens who are in need.
There's the challenge of immigration
and the plight of the unemployed,
the underemployed and the uninsured,
along with the growing number
of poor children in our land of plenty.

At church I'm reminded again and again
of the words and works of Jesus and the prophets,
yet I come away having heard very little said
about what can be done to achieve justice
in our economically-unjust nation.

Instead of working to rectify the system
that has created a bottomless pit of poverty,
the church passes out holiday charity baskets
and deludes itself into thinking
that this is enough to fulfill the teachings
of Jesus, who was born in poverty
and died in poverty.
The clergy do not wish to offend
the wealthy parishioners who give fat checks
for buildings and budgets

and they certainly do not want to risk
losing their tax-free status
by speaking directly to the sin
that is the foundation of all evil in this society
that has seemingly lost its soul to Mammon.

Where is the place of *applied theology* in today's church?
Then and now—a troublesome dichotomy.

Poverty entails fear and stress and sometimes depression. It means a thousand petty humiliations and hardships.

— J. K. Rowling

GOD OF THE STATUS QUO?

Many, both rich and poor,
might very well believe that,
economically, things in our nation
are just what God intended.
God willed it, as Los Pobres
in Latin America believed
before Liberation Theology
challenged that age-old assumption
and made obsolete the traditional
interpretations of biblical texts
that failed to apply the radical
nature of the teachings of Jesus
and the Hebrew prophets.

The story of the Exodus is not only
a story about the children of Israel
escaping from the tyranny of Egypt.
It is also a paradigm for
oppressed people of all times.

Preaching Good News to the poor
and liberation of those who are oppressed
has far-reaching application to the current
economic disparity between the rich and poor.
Jesus is not limiting salvation
to individual, isolated souls, but extending
true liberation for all humankind
from bondage and servitude to any empire
that rewards the rich at the expense of the poor.

It is those who profit most
who are the creators
and sustainers of the status quo,
and they are not gods.
They are demons who make deals
under the ruse of law and order.
They are purveyors of systemic violence.

I cannot believe in a God who would order
an economic system in which only a few
would have huge surpluses
while tens of millions do without.
I cannot believe that God is pleased
with our status quo.

WHAT CAN CHANGE
THE STATUS QUO?

How can we possibly become a more just nation
in light of the political and economic power
that the wealthiest wield
against the interests of the majority
of the citizens of this country?
America's economic health and the welfare
of most of her inhabitants
lie in the hands of that tiny fraction
of citizens—the super rich—
who have easy access to those
who enact policies within the halls of Congress.

Capitalism is failing and so is democracy.
The votes of 2008, votes for Change,
have been rendered null and void
by the corporate interests
whose power affords them free reign
to continue to capitalize
on an economic system
that is nothing less
than institutionalized violence.

So what are those who have been left out
of the equation of power to do
when both democracy and capitalism
have lost their relevance to the millions
who live without health insurance,
those tens of millions who try to manage
their lives on substandard wages,

extremely substandard wages
when compared to the exorbitant wages
of our corporate ruling class?
That "elite" class draws wages
that are 300 times the earnings
of the average American worker.

How long will it take for enough of us
to realize that bipartisanship and civility
can no longer bring about the change
that is required
to secure the common good?

ROBIN HOOD AT CHRISTMAS

What if we made Robin Hood
the new symbol
of Christmas in America?
What if we made him
the main character
in our Christmas pageants?
Think of it:
a jolly yuletide vagabond
who takes from the rich
to give to the poor.

What a hero!
The shrieking of the wealthy
might at last reveal the extent
of their insatiable greed.
Lavishing goods on the poor
might become a paradigm
for those of us who already
have more than enough.
And a promise of equity
on at least one occasion of the year
might make life more bearable
for those in poverty.

Poverty is a noose that strangles humility and breeds disrespect for God and man.

— Native American Proverb

DOES GOD PROVIDE?

Who has the means to live
without concern for food,
for a place to dwell, for clothing,
for security for tomorrow's needs?
Does God truly provide all of these
without our concentrated effort,
as Jesus suggested?

The economic conditions
of the vast majority in our world
suggest that either God does not provide
as promised, or that his purposes
have been thwarted by the greed
of those who possess power.
Or perhaps his purposes
have been thwarted by apathy
on the part of those who
profess to be his followers
but do not practice what they preach.

In order for there to be
a Kingdom of God on earth,
those who worship Sunday after Sunday
should leave their sanctuaries
with the intent to carry out God's plan
so that the greedy few
would no longer be allowed
to possess the goods that rightly
belong to *all* of God's children.

ALL GOD'S CHILDREN

Are we not all God's children
and are we not all equal
in the sight of our Creator?
If we are,
if we are,
then why must we be consigned
to exist in ways
that are not sustainable
for so many of God's children?

Is this God's family?
Is this the home
that our Creator intended?
We *are* all God's children.
We *are* all equal
in the sight of our Creator.
So we should be entitled
to equal portions
of the earth's resources.

Let us pledge to live
as sisters and brothers,
cognizant of the sins of greed
and the plight of those in want.
Let us live soberly,
sensibly, simply
so that we can all truly share
in the goodness of God's creation.

WHAT WE ARE

What we are,
what we have,
what we are,
what we own.
Into this world
we came with nothing.

What we are,
what we earn,
what we are,
what was given to us,
what we are,
what was taken away.
Into this world
we came with nothing.

What we are,
what are we worth?
It is not
what we leave behind,
what we are
when we die.

What we are is that
which was given to us
before we came,
not the luggage we acquired
in the journey
from the cradle to the grave.

RICH MAN'S BURIAL

Today a very wealthy man
was buried in much the same manner
as many others are laid to rest,
with the exception that this man
was buried in his magnificent limousine
loaded with possessions he had garnered
during his very successful career.
Inside the limo were expensive watches,
rings, rare works of art and sculpture,
as well as photos of the homes
and estates he had once owned.

Another exception of this interment
was that there were no mourners, not one,
for he had devoted all of his time,
his passion and his efforts
to the acquisition of possessions.
And so today he had with him
all that had brought him comfort and pleasure.
There was no one to grieve his passing
for he will not be missed.

The game is over. We lost. The corporate state will continue its inexorable advance until two-thirds of the nation is locked into a desperate, permanent under-class. Most Americans will struggle to make a living while the Blankfeins and our political elites wallow in the decadence and greed of the Forbidden City and Versailles. These elites do not have a vision. They know only one word—more.

— Chris Hedges

WHEN ALL IS SAID AND DONE

When history finally tells its truth,
this is what will be asked regarding our lives:
"Where did you stand and what did you say
in the heat of the battle for justice?"
No one knows what the final judgment will be.
Yet there are issues at stake
today and in our near future,
issues that affect the lives of millions
of people who ask for someone
to speak on their behalf,
to be their advocate in the halls of power,
to make life more bearable,
more humane,
more civilized.

The inequity between the haves
and the have-nots is increasing
to the point of spinning out of control.
The public good is being
bargained away for private gain.

Where do you think God
would be in this debate?
Just a hunch:
on the side of the oppressed.
So why isn't there more of a moral outcry
from those who profess to believe
and follow God's biblical principles?
This is not just about politics.
It is about doing what benefits the many
and not just the privileged few.

The healthcare debate was one-sided,
lopsided to the advantage
of those who desire
to make much more money
from the already-shrinking coffers
of the diminishing middle class
and the uninsured poor.
So the healthcare legislation
that finally made its way through Congress
is not what it should have been,
what it could have been
if the common good had been
more a part of the conversation
than the welfare of the insurance companies,
the pharmaceutical companies
and their vast armies of lobbyists.

But the legislation is a beginning,
a step toward the reform
that is so desperately needed.
Should it be repealed,
the repeal will not only be a result
of the work of conservative politicians
who speak and act at the behest
of the healthcare corporations.
It will also be the result of SILENCE,
the STONE-COLD SILENCE
of people who consider themselves
morally upright and just
but are apathetic regarding the plight of others
because they themselves are covered.

Who else will be to blame?
Ministers who know their scriptures
but do not believe
it is in their best interests
to bring this moral issue
to the attention of their congregations.

The influence of money and power
may very well win this battle,
yet history will someday
judge us all
for what we did and said
and what we did not do and say
when the time was ripe for change,
ripe for justice.

PRAYER FOR THE CHILDREN

IN HONOR OF THE LEGACY OF WALTER RAUSCHENBUSCH

Dear Creator,
we acknowledge in this moment
that we are all your children,
without regard to race, creed,
nationality or faith orientation.

And we also acknowledge
your special concern for the
impoverished, the oppressed,
the hungry, the infirmed children,
both here in our nation
and throughout the earth.

Our prayer is for the insight
to see all the wounded
children of this earth
with eyes of compassion,
just as Jesus saw them,
to literally *suffer with*
those who are victimized
by the forces of structural evil.

We confess our own complicity,
our complacency, our apathy
toward a world that produces
so great a disparity as now exists
between those of us
who are privileged
and those whose lives are

continually in peril
due to lack of their day's manna.

We ask forgiveness
because we realize our profession
and our beliefs
are not always matched by practice—
the practice of justice,
the practice of peace.

We ask for courage
to do the deeds,
to take the steps
that will truly make the world
a community
in which we cast aside
the idols of power,
the idols of empire,
the idols of militarism,
the idols of world supremacy,
the idols of greed.

We acknowledge
your abundant Grace that is
offered to children everywhere.
May we live our lives
as an expression of gratitude
for that unconditional love
as we love unconditionally
all the children of the world.